My Silent Reveries

A Collection of Tanka Poetry: Where Trauma, Love and Hope Can Coexist

Claudia Gonzalez

BookLeaf Publishing

India | USA | UK

Made with ❤ on the BookLeaf Publishing Platform

www.bookleafpub.in

www.bookleafpub.com

Dedication

For the neurodiverse empath souls,
who feel deeply, hurt more,
yet shine with boundless creativity,
radiating light and inspiring with
extraordinary abilities.

Magali, Duke, and Blue, thank you
for lifting me up when feeling too much becomes too
difficult.

Preface

In "My Silent Reveries," I invite you on a journey through the delicate tapestry of human experience, woven with threads of trauma, love, and hope. This collection of Tanka poetry delves into the profound depths of our inner worlds, acknowledging that we are all a little broken. Yet, it is within these fractures that the light of love and hope finds its way, illuminating our path and lifting us up.

Life is a complex dance of emotions, where past traumas coexist with the healing power of love and the promise of hope. As we navigate these intertwining currents, we can heal our inner child, finding solace in the glimmers that make this life worthwhile. For those of us who feel deeply, whether as empaths or neurodiverse souls, the lows may be profound, but so too are the heights of our joys.

"My Silent Reveries" celebrates the beauty of this coexistence, reminding us that it is perfectly okay to carry all these emotions within us. It is through embracing our vulnerabilities, our capacity for love, and our unwavering hope that we find the strength to rise above. This collection is a testament to the resilience of the human spirit and the transformative power of poetry.

May these verses resonate with your heart and soul,
offering comfort, inspiration, and a sense of connection.
Thank you for joining me on this poetic journey.

Acknowledgements

I want to extend my heartfelt thanks to all the souls I've encountered along my journey. Each of you has played a part in shaping my memories, my life, and my path, bringing me to who I am today. This book is a testament to trauma, love, hope, and the beauty of healing.

To those who were part of my childhood and the healing of my inner child, I acknowledge your impact. Together, we celebrate the beauty of healing and the ability to coexist with these experiences in our lives. Thank you.

1. Trauma:

Embracing the Shadows

Life can be so tough. There, I've admitted it. Sometimes, I feel like shouting it from the mountaintops with arms raised, "WHY ME?" "I didn't deserve this!" An invisible, crippling pain. Debilitating wounds so deep. Fragile scars that no longer bleed. Constant reminders of the hell I've endured. This can't be erased. THIS...is the trauma I carry.

constant reminders
entangled in my happy
please just let me breathe

1. War

living in battle
haunted whispers taunt my dreams
all good things desired
are questioned by these sad thoughts
am I deserving of peace

1. Haunted

so young to be bruised
trauma held my hand since birth
no consent given
it still haunts me years later
what would I be without you

1. Heavy

how I miss this me
that I've never met, you see
it's the part that you
took away and burdened me
weight crushing down my chest

1. Tango

i danced with the devil
kept my rhythm, played the part
protected my heart
we no longer dance these days
i ended that song, my terms

1. Nostalgist

inner me, rest please
why do my saddest memories
replay in my mind
a cassette stuck on rewind
help me move forward

1. Fragile

you are beautiful
every scar the beaten path
glimpse of tragic past
a child not ready for that
you survived, what no one should

2. Worthy of Love: Taking it All In

The lows can be profound, but so too are the height of our joys. The human experience does this thing, where it's so easy to dwell on the dark instead of looking around to even just acknowledge the amount of light that surrounds us. Yes, we've been through heart break, moments we wish we could erase, and the reality is that people's actions will hurt us; but not everyone is the same. Somewhere, someone loves you. A love so deep it hurts, so pure it's priceless. You are meant to be loved. Embrace it. Look around you. It's there. In every smile, kiss, warm embrace, "thank you" and kind gesture. You are so worthy. Love YOU.

fractured soul, look up
you are everything and more
light and love are yours

2. Divinity

our lives intertwined
branches of a willow tree
the memories deep rooted
ancestors guiding our path
journey planted, meant to be

2. Breathless

souls tied, you call me
eyes on you, my heart could cry
exhilarating
like storms lighting up the sky
my world needs your lasting shine

2. Blessed

an answered prayer
to my truest love, thank you
beautiful secret
lost in depths of endless dreams
i've loved you...every lifetime

2. Soulmate

invisible string
always held us together
was perfectly timed
altered moments, stars aligned
our destiny a blessing

2. Mamá

you overcame that
your strength infused every word
you held your ground firm
an everlasting beauty
a legacy of true love

2. Roots

14

unbreakable bond
reflections of tragic past
healing together
the intricately woven
threads in timeless tapestries

3. Unwavering Hope: Finding the Strength to Rise Above

As we navigate these intertwining currents, we can heal our inner child, finding solace in the glimmers that make this life worthwhile. Fleeting moments don't have to leave you by. Romanticize the mundane. This here, right now, is yours to make. This weight you carry has made you stronger, kinder, and more prepared. You are ready to create the beautiful, enriching life you deserve. Wear your coziest attire, savor your favorite drink, dance along as your favorite notes engulf your soul. Revel in the vastness of the sparkling ocean beneath the setting sky. Laugh until you cry and honor that pure heart you wear on your long, cozy sleeve. With the help of the love that surrounds you and your glimmers of hope, you can begin to heal knowing it is perfectly okay to carry all these emotions within us.

these flowing rivers
cleanse and heal your wounded heart
grounded by nature

3. Harmony

16

music feeds your soul
your innermost scars cradled
notes that you create,
you choreograph, you sing,
bring life to your universe

3. Magical

dancing breath on this
chilly and bright November
golden hour, photo shoots
dewy days, mystical scenes
mornings like this forever

3. Alien

far from planet Earth
i live in a universe
all things amplified
here we live and breathe feeling
hold on to those that understand

3. Wildflower

a rugged beauty
glimmers of hope embrace you
thistles and daisies
basket filled with dainty weeds
peaceful, collected memories

3. Blue

white whispy whiskers
eyes that reflect pure, true soul
paws perfectly mine
your lifetime my favorite view
i'll look for you in rainbows

3. Breathe

21

stronger, more mindful
be proud of who you've become
slowly living now
relive treasured memories
release what doesn't serve you

It will be okay.